# Seas & OCEANS

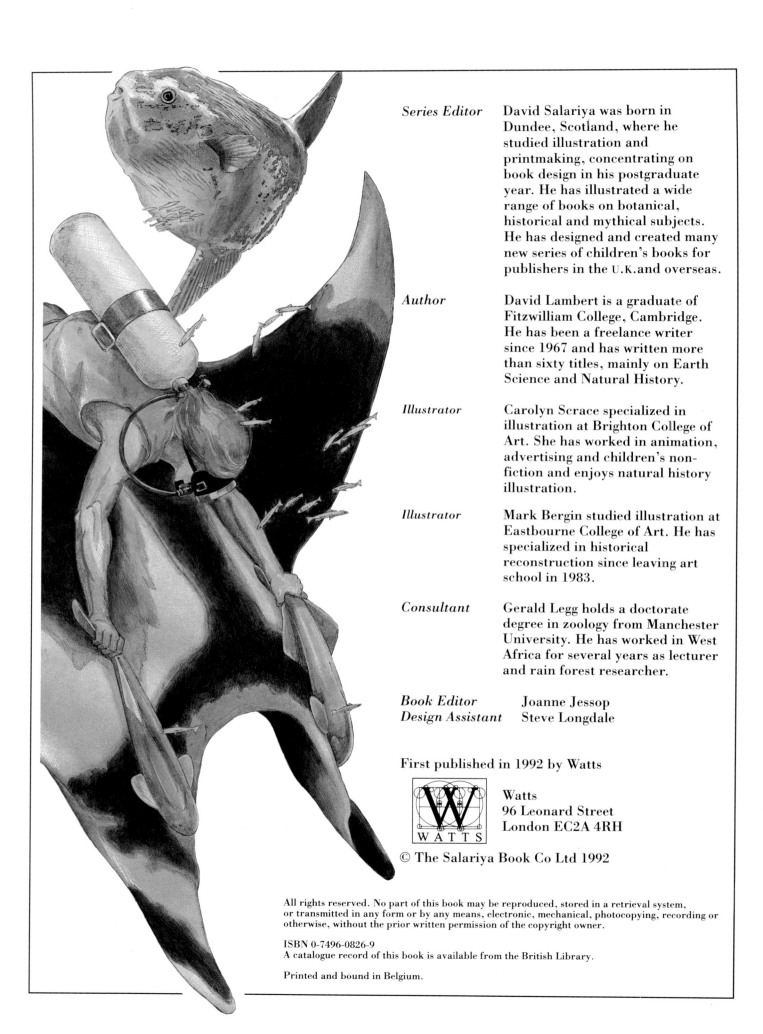

**Series Editor** — David Salariya was born in Dundee, Scotland, where he studied illustration and printmaking, concentrating on book design in his postgraduate year. He has illustrated a wide range of books on botanical, historical and mythical subjects. He has designed and created many new series of children's books for publishers in the U.K. and overseas.

**Author** — David Lambert is a graduate of Fitzwilliam College, Cambridge. He has been a freelance writer since 1967 and has written more than sixty titles, mainly on Earth Science and Natural History.

**Illustrator** — Carolyn Scrace specialized in illustration at Brighton College of Art. She has worked in animation, advertising and children's non-fiction and enjoys natural history illustration.

**Illustrator** — Mark Bergin studied illustration at Eastbourne College of Art. He has specialized in historical reconstruction since leaving art school in 1983.

**Consultant** — Gerald Legg holds a doctorate degree in zoology from Manchester University. He has worked in West Africa for several years as lecturer and rain forest researcher.

**Book Editor** — Joanne Jessop
**Design Assistant** — Steve Longdale

First published in 1992 by Watts

Watts
96 Leonard Street
London EC2A 4RH

© The Salariya Book Co Ltd 1992

ISBN 0-7496-0826-9
A catalogue record of this book is available from the British Library.

Printed and bound in Belgium.

# NEW View Seas & OCEANS

Written by
**DAVID LAMBERT**

Illustrated by
**CAROLYN SCRACE & MARK BERGIN**

Created & Designed by
**DAVID SALARIYA**

# A WATTS BOOK

London • New York • Sydney • Toronto

# CONTENTS

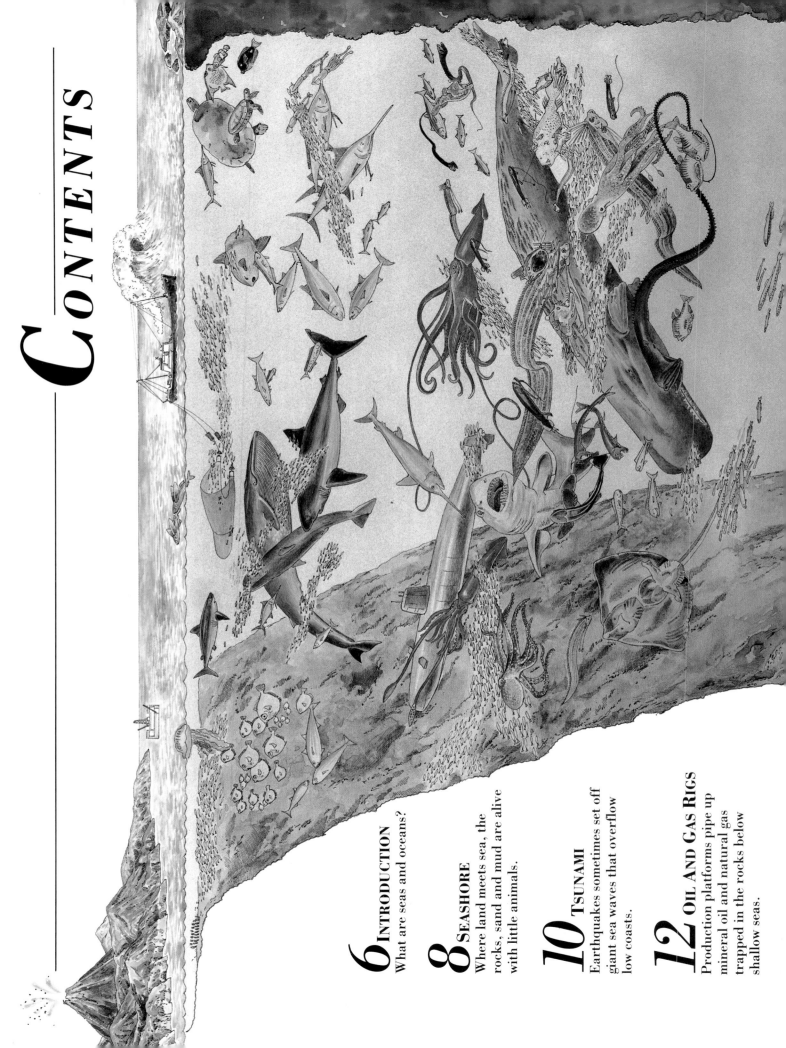

# INTRODUCTION

*L*iving on land, we easily forget that salty sea water covers most of the Earth. Four great connected hollows in the Earth's surface contain the Arctic, Atlantic, Indian and Pacific oceans. The Pacific alone is big enough to hold every continent, and its deepest part could cover the highest mountain peak on land with more than 2000 metres of water. If you could drain the oceans, the Earth's largest feature seen from space would be the mountain range that runs along the ocean basins. This range is more than 60,000 kilometres long, by far the longest in the world. Large areas of partly enclosed ocean form most of the world's seas; a few are completely landlocked. Seas and oceans contain 97 per cent of the world's water and cover about 70 per cent of the Earth's surface.

To early sailors, oceanic storms and reefs were a frequent cause of deadly shipwreck. Yet people have long dared to make the sea a highway and a source of food. Now, sturdy fishing boats range into wild polar waters; engineers pump oil and gas from seabed wells; modern nuclear submarines can circle the world below the surface of the oceans; and underwater explorers in pressure-proof boats plunge kilometres deep.

Each layer of the sea is home to living things suited to that level. Only the sunlit surface is bright enough for plants to grow. Deeper down, little lights gleam, produced by creatures that live in perpetual darkness and almost freezing temperatures, under pressure that would burst a diver's lungs.

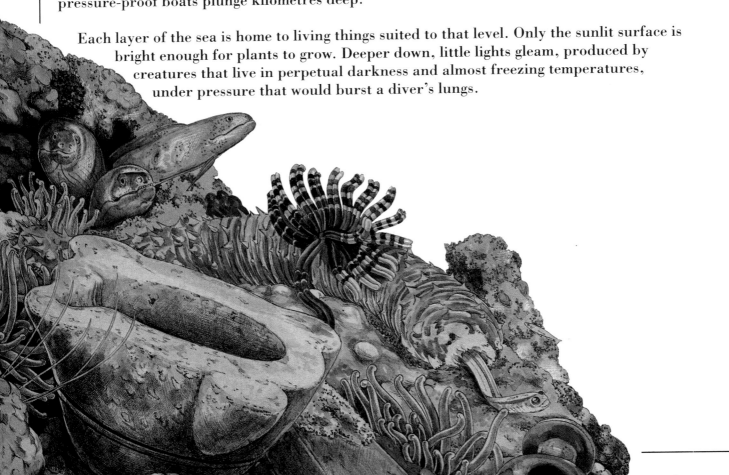

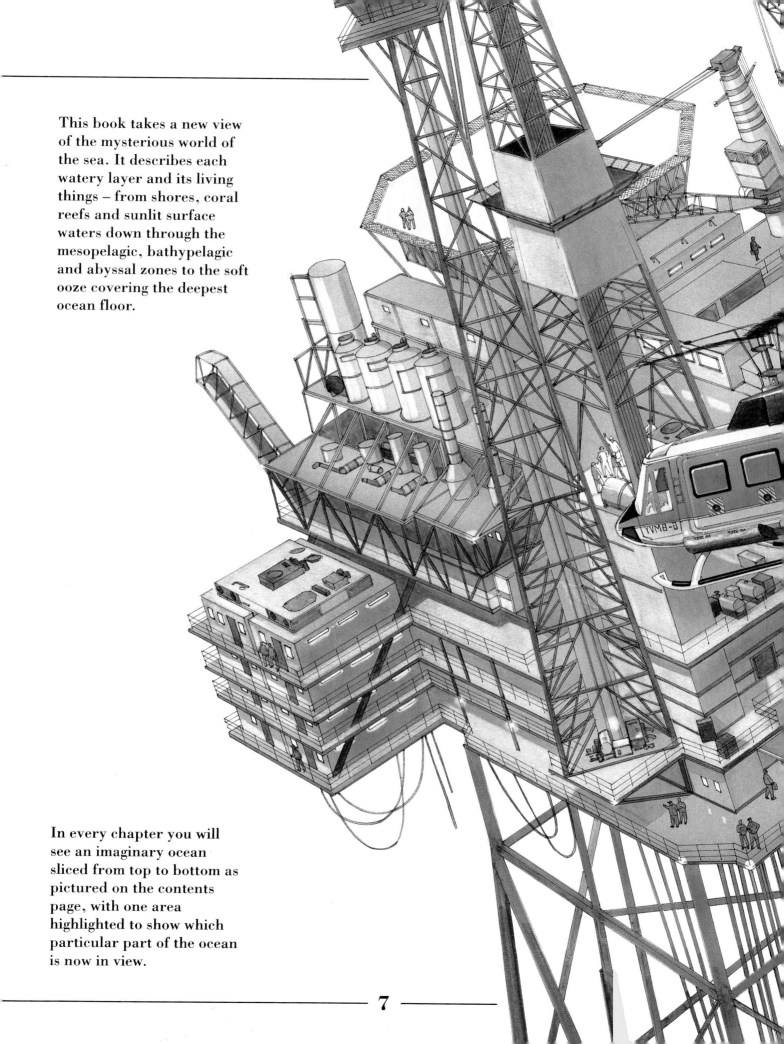

This book takes a new view of the mysterious world of the sea. It describes each watery layer and its living things – from shores, coral reefs and sunlit surface waters down through the mesopelagic, bathypelagic and abyssal zones to the soft ooze covering the deepest ocean floor.

In every chapter you will see an imaginary ocean sliced from top to bottom as pictured on the contents page, with one area highlighted to show which particular part of the ocean is now in view.

• Twice a day the water in the sea rises and twice a day it goes back. These changing tides are caused by the pull of the Sun and the Moon on different parts of the Earth.

• A starfish (19) has a mouth below its middle. It uses its arms to pull apart a mussel shell, then pushes its stomach out through its mouth to digest the mussel's soft body (20).

# SEASHORE

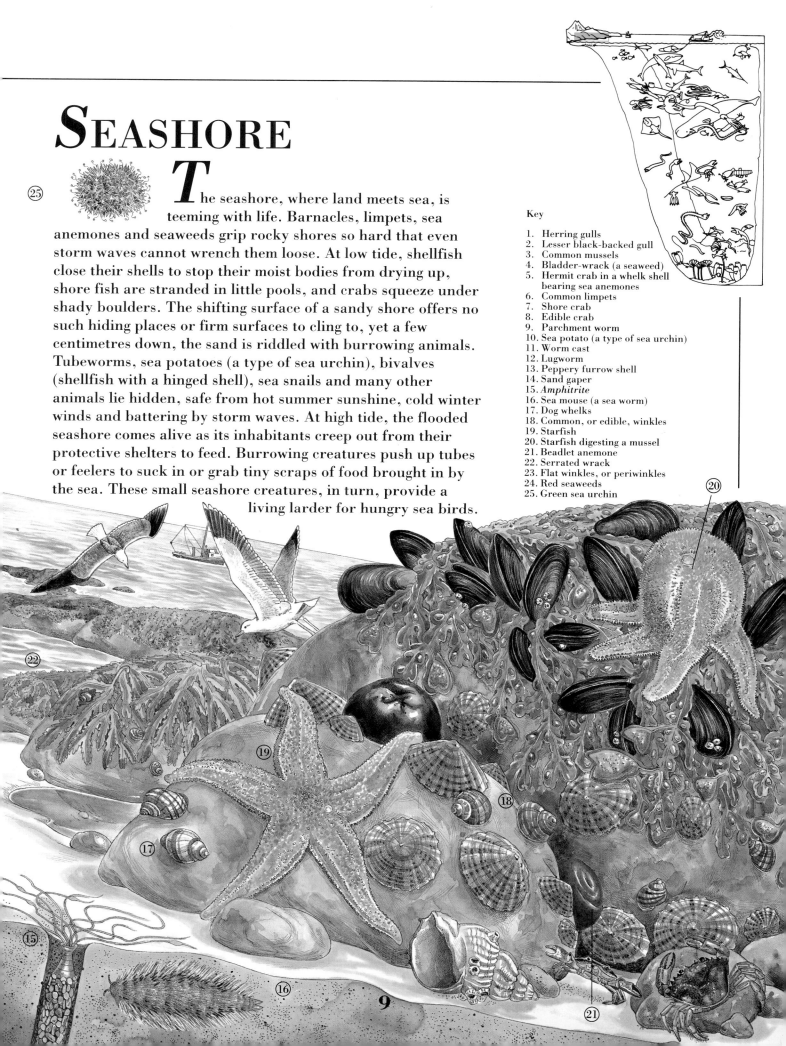

*T*he seashore, where land meets sea, is teeming with life. Barnacles, limpets, sea anemones and seaweeds grip rocky shores so hard that even storm waves cannot wrench them loose. At low tide, shellfish close their shells to stop their moist bodies from drying up, shore fish are stranded in little pools, and crabs squeeze under shady boulders. The shifting surface of a sandy shore offers no such hiding places or firm surfaces to cling to, yet a few centimetres down, the sand is riddled with burrowing animals. Tubeworms, sea potatoes (a type of sea urchin), bivalves (shellfish with a hinged shell), sea snails and many other animals lie hidden, safe from hot summer sunshine, cold winter winds and battering by storm waves. At high tide, the flooded seashore comes alive as its inhabitants creep out from their protective shelters to feed. Burrowing creatures push up tubes or feelers to suck in or grab tiny scraps of food brought in by the sea. These small seashore creatures, in turn, provide a living larder for hungry sea birds.

**Key**

1. Herring gulls
2. Lesser black-backed gull
3. Common mussels
4. Bladder-wrack (a seaweed)
5. Hermit crab in a whelk shell bearing sea anemones
6. Common limpets
7. Shore crab
8. Edible crab
9. Parchment worm
10. Sea potato (a type of sea urchin)
11. Worm cast
12. Lugworm
13. Peppery furrow shell
14. Sand gaper
15. *Amphitrite*
16. Sea mouse (a sea worm)
17. Dog whelks
18. Common, or edible, winkles
19. Starfish
20. Starfish digesting a mussel
21. Beadlet anemone
22. Serrated wrack
23. Flat winkles, or periwinkles
24. Red seaweeds
25. Green sea urchin

9

# TSUNAMI

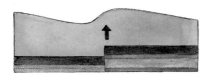

*Tsu* is Japanese for "overflowing"; *nami* means "wave". A tsunami is a giant sea wave that overflows the land. People often call tsunamis "tidal waves", but they have nothing to do with the sea's slow tidal rise and fall. Tsunamis are unleashed by sudden movements of the seabed caused by earthquakes or volcanic eruptions. As the seabed shifts up or down it disturbs the layers of water above (see diagram above). One after another, huge ripples speed out in all directions across the ocean surface. Each of these tsunamis can streak across an ocean almost as fast as a jet plane. At first, the wave is less than a metre high – so low that ships' crews do not even feel it pass. As the tsunami approaches a coastline, the water piles up. Tsunamis have been known to rise 18 metres on flat, low-lying shores and more than 30 metres at the head of V-shaped inlets. The water sweeps inshore, smashing buildings, uprooting trees and tossing cars around like tiny toys.

This picture shows the likely damage done when tsunamis hit a coastal city reeling from an earthquake. Such a double blow struck Lisbon, the capital of Portugal, in November 1755. To escape collapsing buildings, crowds streamed out onto the quay only to be drowned by the giant waves that started rushing in. Some estimates suggest that 60,000 people lost their lives.

- One Hawaiian island bears traces from prehistoric times of a giant wave 300 metres high.

- In 1771 a tsunami that hit one of the Ryukyu Islands south of Japan tossed a 725-tonne block of coral 2.5 kilometres inland.

- In 1946 a tsunami caused by an earthquake off Alaska was 17 metres high when it hit the Hawaiian islands.

- In 1883 the volcanic eruption of the island of Krakatoa in Indonesia created a huge tsunami. It was more than 30 metres tall when it crashed into the islands of Java and Sumatra. When the waves subsided, one large ship was found a kilometre inland.

# *O*IL AND GAS RIGS

*A*rtificial islands peep above the water in parts of the North Sea, Arctic Ocean, Gulf of Mexico and other offshore waters. The islands are the tops of oil and gas rigs rising from the seabed. Most rigs were built on land as steel or concrete towers, then towed out by tugs and erected on the ocean floor. Many rigs stand in fairly shallow water, but some rise through water more than 200 metres deep.

On a big rig's fixed platform, perched above the highest waves, are the living quarters for hundreds of workers, as well as the equipment they need to drill for petroleum oil and natural gas trapped below the seabed. Towering above the platform is the derrick, which holds all the drilling machinery. There are enough metal tubes stacked on the platform to line a well several thousand metres deep. Tubes may be sent out in various directions from a single platform in order to drain the oil or gas from a large area. Generators on board the platform supply all the power needed to run the equipment and service the living quarters. Workers and supplies are transported to and from the rig by boat or by helicopter, which sets down on a special landing pad. A big fixed platform is like a small industrial town set in the sea.

Key

1. Telecommunications tower
2. Crane
3. Metal tubes to line the well
4. Crane
5. Helipad
6. Drilling derrick
7. Flare boom for burning off excess gas
8. Gangplank, can be lowered onto support vessels when they arrive at the platform
9. Living quarters
10. Electrical communications cables
11. Drill head area
12. Tubes carrying oil from below the seabed

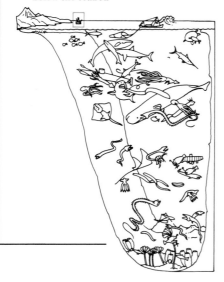

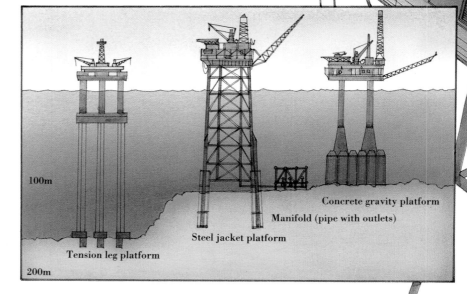

100m

200m

Tension leg platform

Steel jacket platform

Manifold (pipe with outlets)

Concrete gravity platform

The tension leg platform is a buoyant platform tethered to the seabed by jointed legs kept in tension by computer-controlled adjustment. The steel jacket platform rests on a frame of steel supports (jackets) pinned to the seabed with steel piles. The concrete gravity platform sits on concrete legs held on the seabed by their great weight.

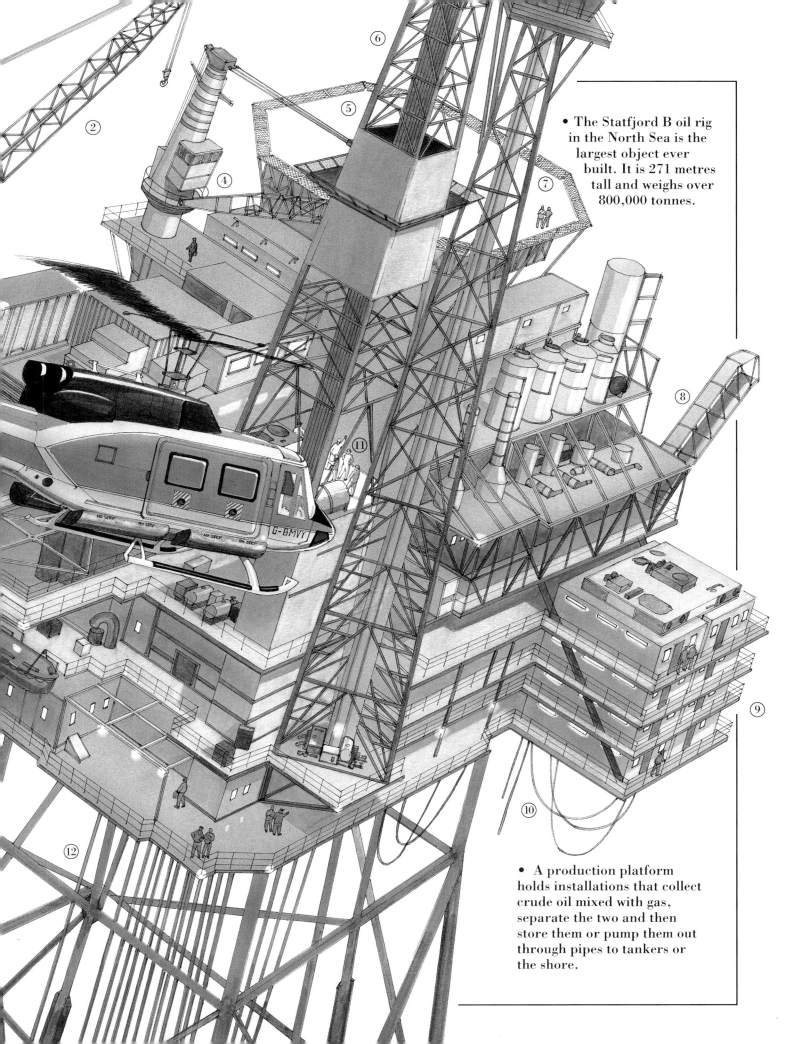

• The Statfjord B oil rig in the North Sea is the largest object ever built. It is 271 metres tall and weighs over 800,000 tonnes.

• A production platform holds installations that collect crude oil mixed with gas, separate the two and then store them or pump them out through pipes to tankers or the shore.

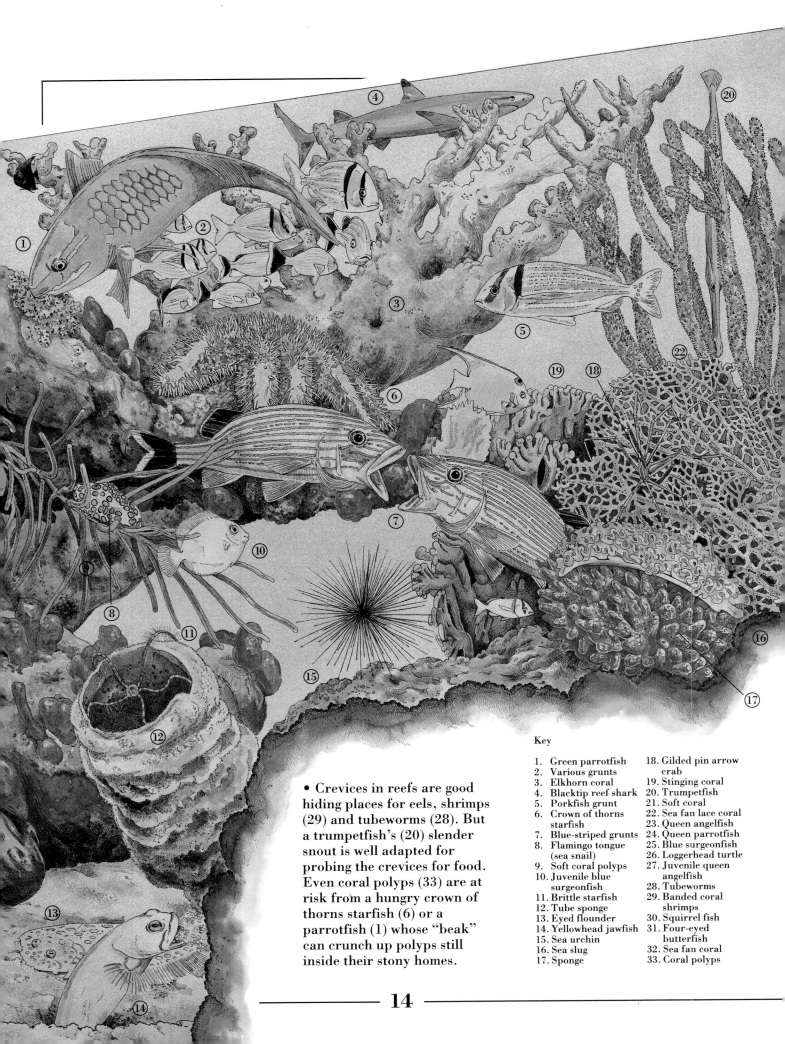

• Crevices in reefs are good hiding places for eels, shrimps (29) and tubeworms (28). But a trumpetfish's (20) slender snout is well adapted for probing the crevices for food. Even coral polyps (33) are at risk from a hungry crown of thorns starfish (6) or a parrotfish (1) whose "beak" can crunch up polyps still inside their stony homes.

Key

1. Green parrotfish
2. Various grunts
3. Elkhorn coral
4. Blacktip reef shark
5. Porkfish grunt
6. Crown of thorns starfish
7. Blue-striped grunts
8. Flamingo tongue (sea snail)
9. Soft coral polyps
10. Juvenile blue surgeonfish
11. Brittle starfish
12. Tube sponge
13. Eyed flounder
14. Yellowhead jawfish
15. Sea urchin
16. Sea slug
17. Sponge
18. Gilded pin arrow crab
19. Stinging coral
20. Trumpetfish
21. Soft coral
22. Sea fan lace coral
23. Queen angelfish
24. Queen parrotfish
25. Blue surgeonfish
26. Loggerhead turtle
27. Juvenile queen angelfish
28. Tubeworms
29. Banded coral shrimps
30. Squirrel fish
31. Four-eyed butterfly
32. Sea fan coral
33. Coral polyps

14

• The Great Barrier Reef off the coast of Australia is 1930 kilometres long, the longest coral reef in the world.

# CORAL REEFS

Coral reefs are rock-like formations found in the warm waters of the tropics. A coral reef is made of the skeletons of billions of tiny coral polyps. Each polyp attaches itself to the reef and builds up a hard, cup-shaped skeleton on the outside of its soft body. It feeds by sending out finger-like tentacles from an opening at the top.

Coral polyps are found only in warm, sunlit water where tiny plants called algae can grow inside the polyps' bodies. Algae give off oxygen, which helps the polyps to breathe. The algae also produce chemicals that help polyps to build their stony skeletons. The outer skeleton grows as the polyp grows. When the coral polyp dies, its skeleton is left and young polyps build new coral cups on top, adding more growth to the reef. Coral grows in a variety of shapes. Some are branched, like elkhorn coral; others are rounded, like brain coral.

# EUPHOTIC ZONE

**S**unlight strong enough for plants to grow penetrates only the top 150 metres or so of the sea. This euphotic, or "well lit", zone takes in a good deal of the continental shelf, which is the shallow sea floor fringing continents. Where upwelling of water brings up natural fertilizers from the seabed, the euphotic zone teems with tiny drifting plants and little animals that feed on plants or one another. Together they form a drifting mass of living organisms called plankton. Planktonic animals provide food for small fish such as anchovies and they, in turn, fall prey to larger, fiercer hunters. Some very large animals like manta rays and the baleen whale feed on plankton directly, guzzling up to several tonnes a day.

The continental shelf provides shelter, food and breeding grounds for many creatures. Moray eels lurk in its rock crevices and hide among shipwrecks. Fish with flattened bodies lie camouflaged on the sandy seabed. Plant-like sea cucumbers eat food scraps that drift down from above. Millions of fish come to the continental shelf each year to mate and spawn.

## Key

1. Flying fish
2. Moray eels
3. Cleaner wrasse
4. Sea cucumber with anemone
5. Pearl fish
6. Doctor's mortar
7. Medicine bottle
8. Sea pens
9. Sawfish
10. Ribs of old ship
11. Pacific angel shark
12. Orange sea cucumber
13. Remains of barrels
14. Remains of casket holding lead balls
15. Cannon barrel
16. Manta ray
17. Remora (clings to larger fish with oval sucking disc on its head)
18. Anchovies
19. Banded sea snake
20. Ocean sunfish

- The sawfish (9) is a big ray with a blade-like snout edged with pointed teeth. It lashes at shoals of fish and roots out creatures that live on the seabed.

- Sea snakes (19) are venomous snakes that swim in the sea, waggling a tail flattened like an oar. Sea snake venom is among the deadliest of poisons.

# DEEP-SEA FISHING

**P**eople still hunt the seas for fish instead of farming most edible species, as we farm sheep or cattle. However, modern deep-sea fishing is much more efficient than in the past when fishing boats cast their nets by guesswork. A modern trawler's captain can spot a shoal of fish nearly 5 kilometres away using an underwater "seeing eye" called sonar (short for SOund Navigation And Ranging). A sonar device sends a pinging sound pulse under the water. Shoals and the seabed return echoes that show up as signals on a meter marked off in different depths. These signals tell the captain exactly where to cast the net. When the catch is hauled on board, it is stored in a refrigerated hold to keep it fresh until the trawler reaches port. Japanese and Russian fishing fleets send out small fishing vessels that bring their catches to big factory ships where the fish are cleaned and stored for weeks at sea.

Deep-sea fishing used to be extremely dangerous. Small fishing vessels were often overwhelmed and sunk in unexpected storms. Now, radioed weather forecasts warn of gales, and modern deep-sea trawlers are strong enough to survive waves that crash down on their decks. That happens quite frequently since some of the richest fishing grounds are in wild Arctic and Antarctic waters.

On these pages a cut-away view shows a modern deep-sea fishing trawler.

### Key

1. Hatch
2. After bipod mast
3. Fish-washing machinery
4. Forward bipod mast
5. Booms
6. Fishing nets
7. Trawl winch
8. Lifeboat
9. Funnel
10. Mast
11. Radar scanner
12. Voice pipe
13. Searchlight
14. Bridge
15. Binnacle (with compass)
16. Steering wheel
17. Engine telegraph
18. Anchor
19. Fresh water
20. Fuel tanks
21. Stores
22. Engine room
23. Galley
24. Crew's quarters
25. Cold store
26. Compressor (for refrigeration unit)
27. Spare fuel tanks
28. Propulsion unit
29. Ship's screw

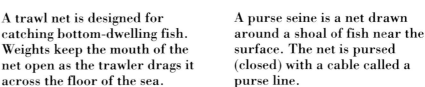

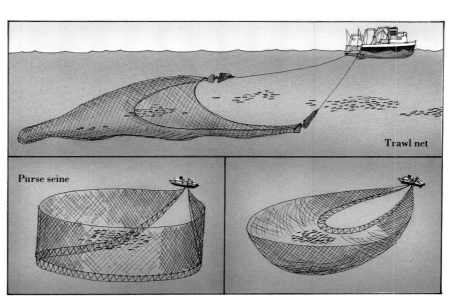

Trawl net

Purse seine

A trawl net is designed for catching bottom-dwelling fish. Weights keep the mouth of the net open as the trawler drags it across the floor of the sea.

A purse seine is a net drawn around a shoal of fish near the surface. The net is pursed (closed) with a cable called a purse line.

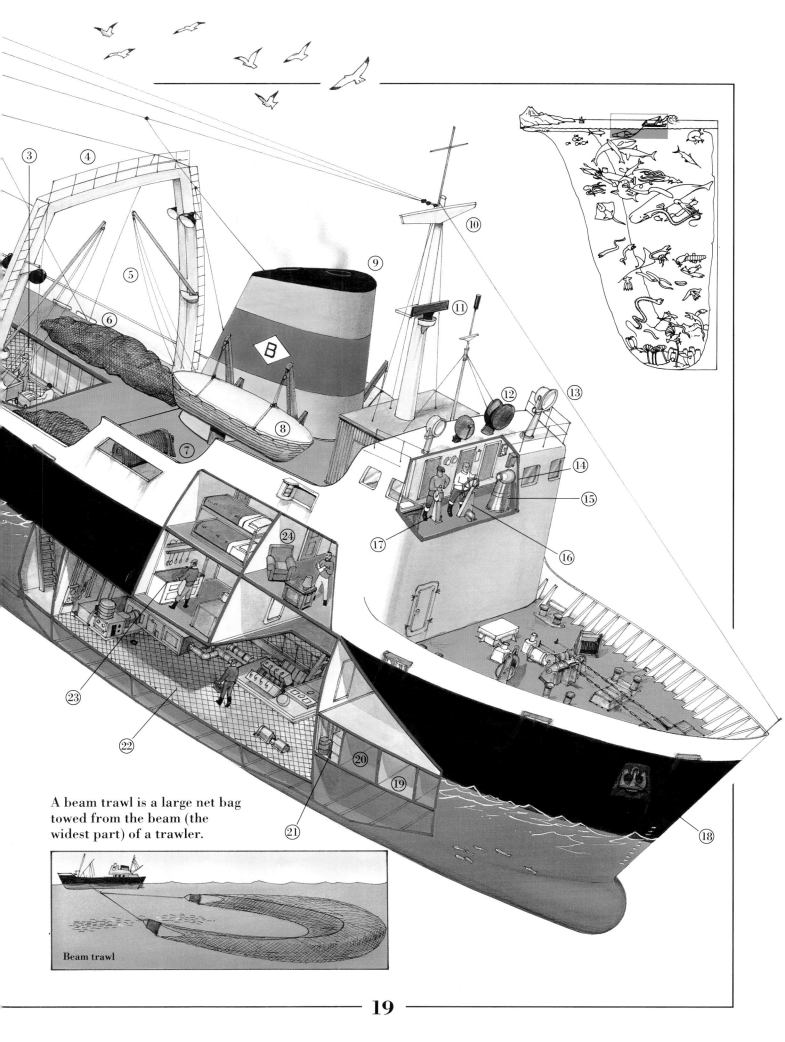

A beam trawl is a large net bag towed from the beam (the widest part) of a trawler.

Beam trawl

# MESOPELAGIC ZONE

**D**eep below the surface of the sea, in the mesopelagic – the "middle open sea" – zone the light fades. At this level, which is between 150 and 1000 metres deep, it is too dark for plants to grow. Creatures survive by eating each other or dead organisms that drift down from above. Sometimes they swim up to feed on organisms living near the surface. Sharks and many other fish swimming at these depths are streamlined hunters that track their prey by scent or by vibrations in the water. Big eyes help the headlamp fish to see in the gloom. Bonitos and other small fish swim in shoals for protection, while squid and jellyfish defend themselves with tentacles. Black fish and red prawns are almost invisible in the gloom. But lantern fish have special body chemicals that produce rows of tiny lights that shine and wink like pearl buttons and help to obscure their shapes. Many fish at this depth have silvery sides that act as mirrors and make the fish difficult to see. Vast swarms of prawns, shrimps and squids migrate up beyond this zone to feed at night when it is difficult for predators to see them.

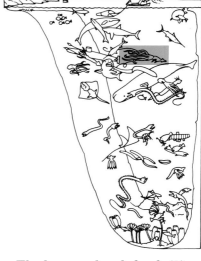

### Key

1. Hammerhead sharks
2. Giant squid
3. Gulper
4. Crustacean
5. Luminous prawn
6. Lantern fish
7. Lantern fish
8. Headlamp fish
9. Sea spider

• The hammerhead shark (1) has a wide, flattened head, more like a spade than a hammer. The head serves as a rudder. The widely spaced nostrils may help the shark to track down prey by scent in dark depths, though hammerheads are usually found in warm, shallow waters.

• The giant squid (2) is the largest mollusc and biggest of all the invertebrates. A giant squid can measure more than 14 metres from its tail to the tip of its longest tentacles.

• Each species of lantern fish (6 and 7) makes its own special light signals. More than 60 per cent of all species of fish living in the mesopelagic zone have lights.

• Most deep-sea prawns and shrimps are luminous. When attacked, some species light up the water with chemicals squirted from a gland below each eye.

# SUBMARINES

**S**ubmarines are ships that can travel both on the sea and deep beneath the surface. When a submarine is ready to submerge, all the openings are closed and the ballast tanks are filled with sea water until the vessel is heavy enough to sink. To rise, high-pressure air is blown into the ballast tanks to force the water out. Wing-like diving planes control how steeply the vessel dives or climbs. A strong hull is needed to withstand the tremendous pressure exerted on it as the submarine descends.

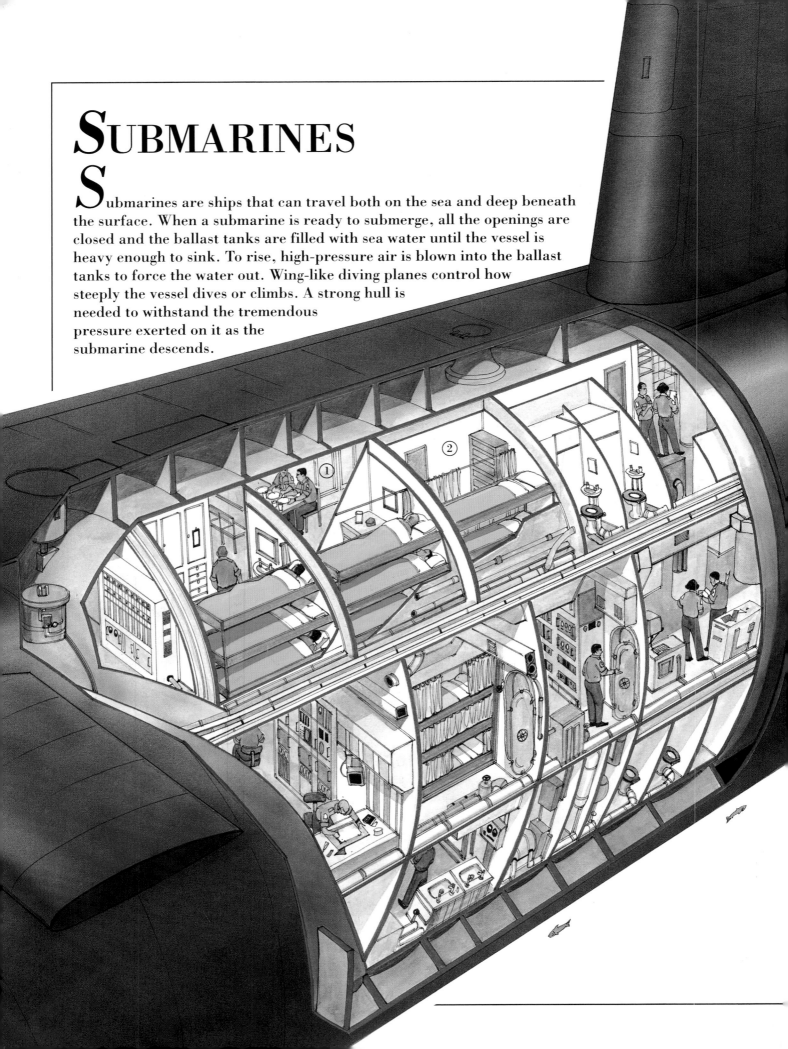

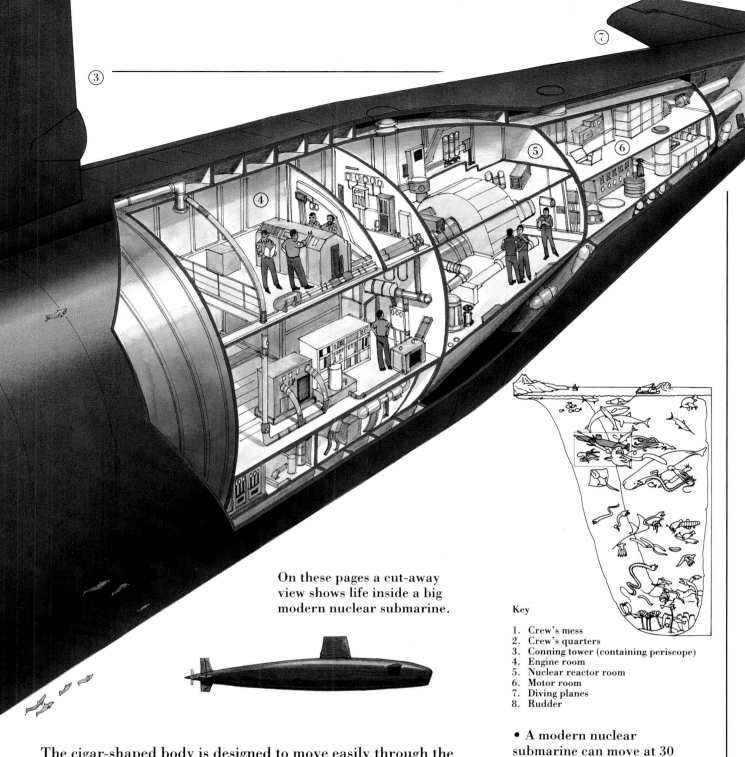

On these pages a cut-away
view shows life inside a big
modern nuclear submarine.

Key

1. Crew's mess
2. Crew's quarters
3. Conning tower (containing periscope)
4. Engine room
5. Nuclear reactor room
6. Motor room
7. Diving planes
8. Rudder

The cigar-shaped body is designed to move easily through the
water. The propeller that drives the submarine forward is
powered by steam, heated either by a diesel-electric or a
nuclear engine. While the submarine is below the surface,
special machines extract from sea water enough fresh drinking
water and supplies of oxygen for a crew of more than a
hundred. A diesel-electric submarine needs air to operate its
diesel engines. When it goes below the surface, the submarine
operates on electricity stored in batteries. It must come up
frequently to re-charge its batteries. A nuclear-powered
submarine, on the other hand, does not need air to run its
power source, so it can stay underwater for months at a time.

• A modern nuclear
submarine can move at 30
knots (55.6 km per hour)
underwater and at 20 knots
(37 km per hour) on the
surface.

• Russia's Typhoon-class
submarines are the world's
largest. These 25,000-tonne
giants are 172 metres long,
which is longer than London's
huge Wembley Stadium, and
twice as wide as the next
widest type of submarines.

# BATHYPELAGIC ZONE

*T*he bathypelagic, or "deep open sea", zone is the pitch-black ocean layer from 1000 to 3000 metres below the surface. Food is scarce down here, so there are fewer creatures than in the mesopelagic layer above and most of the fish grow no bigger than a human hand. Fish of the bathypelagic zone tend to have weak, flabby bodies; they wait in ambush for passing victims rather than using up too much energy chasing the scarce food supply. The deep-sea angler fish even attracts its prey with a light organ - a "bait" - that glows at the top of a "fishing rod" growing out of its head. The gulper can swallow fish larger than itself. Its bag-like, elastic stomach helps it to make the most of the few meals that come its way. Much larger, stronger swimmers sometimes visit the bathypelagic zone. These include giant squids and ribbon-shaped oarfish the length of a bus. Sperm whales weighing more than 30 tonnes sometimes lie on the ocean floor at depths up to 1000 metres, waiting for giant squids.

Key

1. Hatchet fish
2. Deep-sea angler (female with males attached)
3. Oarfish
4. Giant squid
5. Squid
6. Gulper
7. Viper fish
8. Sperm whales
9. Sperm whale calf

• The viper fish (7) has such long teeth that they remain outside when it closes its mouth.

• The hatchet fish (1) get its name from a deep, narrow belly like a hatchet blade and tail like a hatchet handle.

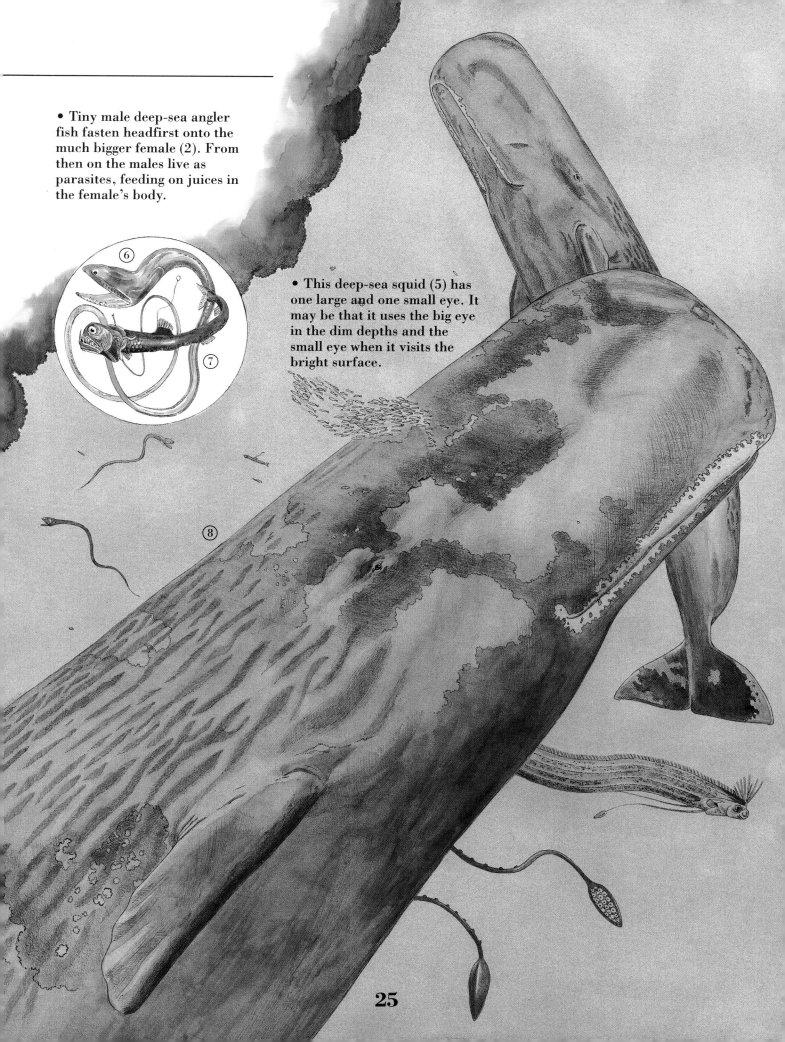

- Tiny male deep-sea angler fish fasten headfirst onto the much bigger female (2). From then on the males live as parasites, feeding on juices in the female's body.

- This deep-sea squid (5) has one large and one small eye. It may be that it uses the big eye in the dim depths and the small eye when it visits the bright surface.

# EXPLORATION

*O*ceans cover seven-tenths of the surface of the Earth, yet we know less about the seabed than about the distant Moon. Until 1960 no one had set eyes on the deep-sea floor itself. Far down, water pressure would crumple any ordinary submarine. Manned exploration needed super-strong underwater craft. At last, in 1960, two men seated in a hollow metal ball with windows, descended nearly 11 kilometres to the bottom of the Marianas Trench in the Pacific Ocean. Even at that great depth, Jacques Piccard and Donald Walsh saw a shrimp and flatfish swimming past.

Their vessel, the *Trieste*, could only sink and rise, but engineers were soon building deep-sea boats that could also

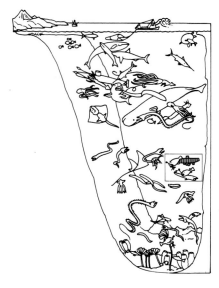

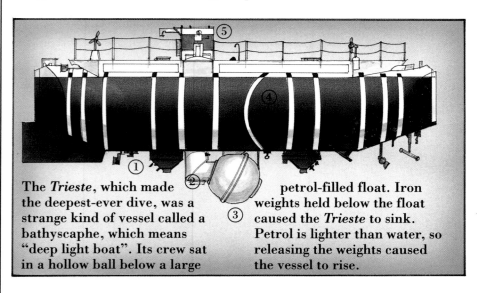

The *Trieste*, which made the deepest-ever dive, was a strange kind of vessel called a bathyscaphe, which means "deep light boat". Its crew sat in a hollow ball below a large petrol-filled float. Iron weights held below the float caused the *Trieste* to sink. Petrol is lighter than water, so releasing the weights caused the vessel to rise.

• If a deep-sea fish is quickly hauled up in a net, the reduced pressure causes its swim bladder to blow up like a balloon.

• In the Marianas Trench, 180,000 tonnes of water pressed on the 9-centimetre-thick walls of the steel ball protecting the *Trieste*'s explorers.

travel forwards and backwards. *Alvin*, an American-built research submersible, is 7 metres long and capable of diving 3650 metres deep. A propeller drives and steers the craft, and motors give it lift. Special instruments help its crew collect samples. In 1977, scientists aboard *Alvin* made remarkable discoveries more than 2 kilometres below the surface on a Pacific Ocean ridge. Jets of scalding water black with chemicals spurted from stony chimneys in the ocean floor. Bacteria nourished by these chemicals provided food for clams, crabs and worms unlike any ever seen before. *Alvin*'s strangest finds included crowds of red-tipped seaworms attached to the seabed and standing up to 3.7 metres tall. Tiny furry tentacles helped them gather tiny particles of food near jets of warm water. Who knows what fresh surprises await explorers of the ocean floor?

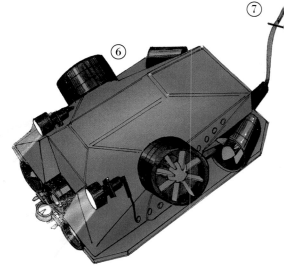

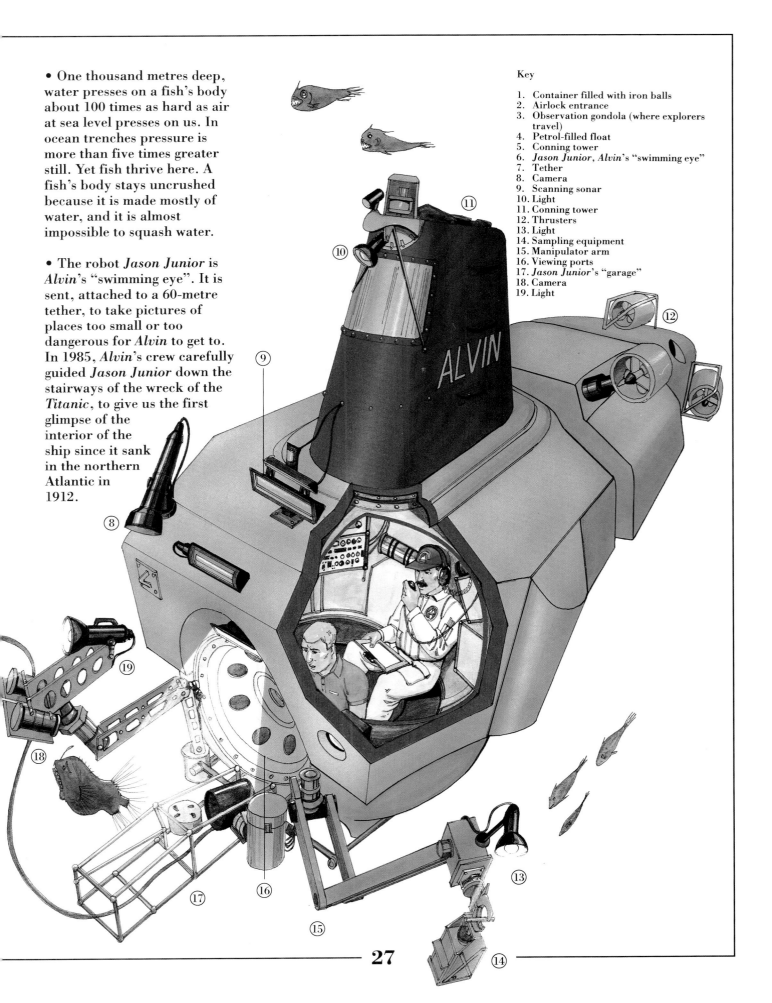

• One thousand metres deep, water presses on a fish's body about 100 times as hard as air at sea level presses on us. In ocean trenches pressure is more than five times greater still. Yet fish thrive here. A fish's body stays uncrushed because it is made mostly of water, and it is almost impossible to squash water.

• The robot *Jason Junior* is *Alvin*'s "swimming eye". It is sent, attached to a 60-metre tether, to take pictures of places too small or too dangerous for *Alvin* to get to. In 1985, *Alvin*'s crew carefully guided *Jason Junior* down the stairways of the wreck of the *Titanic*, to give us the first glimpse of the interior of the ship since it sank in the northern Atlantic in 1912.

Key

1. Container filled with iron balls
2. Airlock entrance
3. Observation gondola (where explorers travel)
4. Petrol-filled float
5. Conning tower
6. *Jason Junior*, *Alvin*'s "swimming eye"
7. Tether
8. Camera
9. Scanning sonar
10. Light
11. Conning tower
12. Thrusters
13. Light
14. Sampling equipment
15. Manipulator arm
16. Viewing ports
17. *Jason Junior*'s "garage"
18. Camera
19. Light

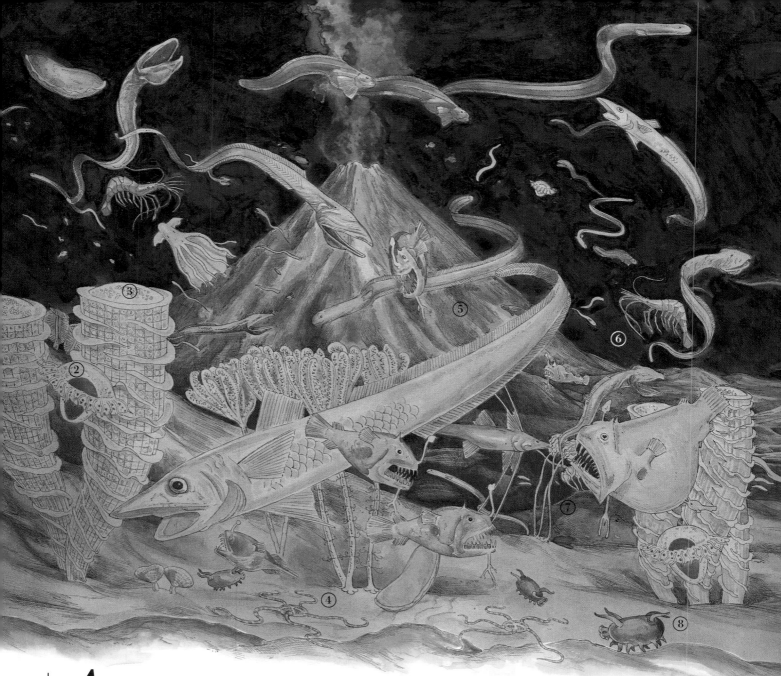

# ABYSSAL ZONE

**W**eird and flimsy fish and other creatures swim or crawl in the everlasting night of the ocean's greatest depths of 3000 to 11,000 metres below the sunlit surface. Down here, in the abyssal zone, the water is almost freezing, and its pressure is immense. Creatures of the abyssal zone all depend for food on dead plants or animals sinking down from water layers several kilometres above. The only light at this depth is the glow from luminous creatures.

The most common bottom dweller is the rat tail – a fish whose body ends in a long filament rather like a rat's tail. The tripod fish rests on its long fin rays. The sea cucumber burrows

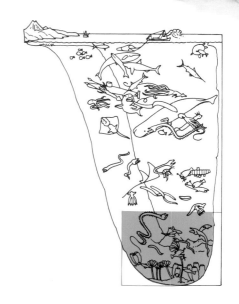

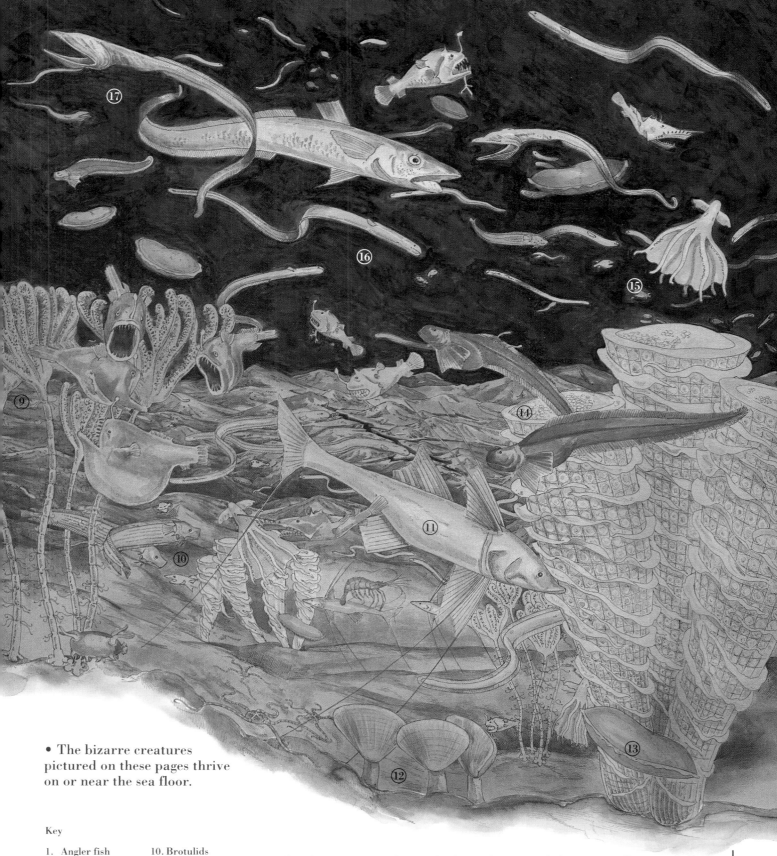

• The bizarre creatures
pictured on these pages thrive
on or near the sea floor.

Key

1. Angler fish
2. Deep-sea jellyfish
3. Venus's flower
   baskets (sponges)
4. Brittle stars
5. Rat tails
6. Deep-sea shrimp
7. Deep-sea anglers
8. Abyssal sea
   cucumbers
9. Stalked crinoids
10. Brotulids
11. Tripod fish
12. Lamp-shells
13. Deep-sea
    swimming
    sea cucumber
14. Sea snails (fish)
15. Abyssal octopus
16. Deep-sea eels
17. Gulpers

for food scraps through the soft ooze of the ocean floor.
The seabed is also home for mollusc-like lamp-shells, or
brachiopods, sponges, and brittle stars and their plant-like
relatives, the stalked crinoids. In places, each square metre of
deep-sea floor is covered by the tangle of arms of as many as
five hundred brittle stars.

# GLOSSARY

**Abyssal zone**
The pitch-black bottom layer of the ocean, about 3000 to 11,000 metres deep.

**Algae**
Simple plants made of one cell or chains or sheets of cells. Algae live in moist places and include seaweeds.

**Baleen whales**
Toothless whales with a comb-like fringe of baleen that hangs down from the upper jaw. The baleen traps small creatures when a whale swims along with its mouth open.

**Bathypelagic zone**
The dark ocean layer 1000 to 3000 metres deep.

**Bivalves**
Clams and other molluscs with a hinged shell they can close or open.

**Brachiopod**
Lamp-shell: a worm-like animal with a pair of bivalve-like shells sprouting from a fleshy stalk.

**Brittle star**
A spindly-armed relative of the starfish.

**Brotulid**
A deep-sea fish with a big head and tapering body fringed with fins. The largest brotulids are about one metre long.

**Continental shelf**
The shallow underwater rim of the continents, averaging about 200 metres deep.

**Coral reef**
A rock-like formation made of the skeletons of billions of tiny sea creatures called coral polyps.

**Crustaceans**
A group of animals that includes shrimps, crabs, barnacles and lobsters. They usually live in water and breathe through gills. They have a hard outer shell and jointed limbs and body.

**Euphotic zone**
The sea's top 150 metres: the sunlit layer where seaweeds and other plants can grow.

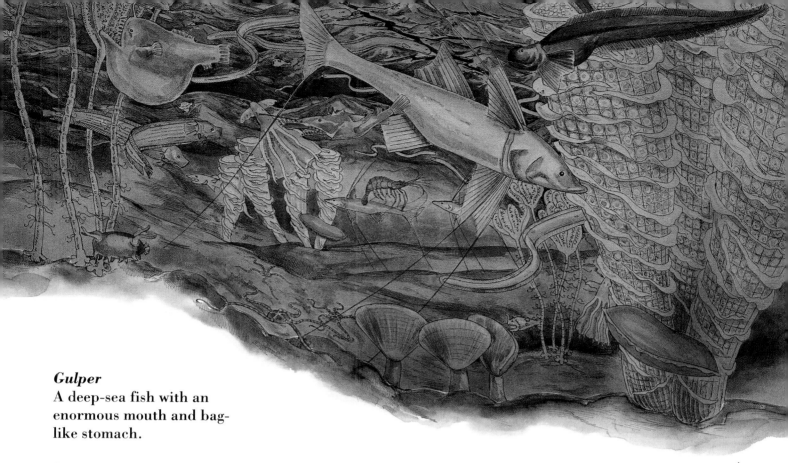

**Gulper**
A deep-sea fish with an enormous mouth and bag-like stomach.

**Invertebrate**
An animal without a backbone.

**Jellyfish**
Jelly-like invertebrates with stinging tentacles that hang down as they drift around on ocean currents.

**Mesopelagic zone**
The "middle open sea" between 150 and 1000 metres deep. Its inhabitants include red prawns and lantern fish.

**Molluscs**
Soft-bodied invertebrates. They include octopuses and squids, and bivalves and snails living in a shell.

**Ray**
A type of fish flattened from top to bottom. Its skeleton is not bony but gristly like a shark's.

**Sea cucumber**
A cucumber-like marine invertebrate with a mouth at one end. Sea cucumbers, sea urchins, starfish and brittle stars are all invertebrates called echinoderms.

**Sea snail**
This name describes any snail that lives in the sea. The same name is also used for a kind of deep-sea fish.

**Sea urchin**
A marine invertebrate that looks like a prickly pincushion. (See also sea cucumber).

**Shark**
A fierce, streamlined carnivorous fish with a gristly skeleton. Sharks eat other fish. Certain kinds of large shark sometimes attack human swimmers.

**Sponge**
A simple hollow-bodied water animal without head, limbs, heart, lungs or other organs. Most sponges live on the seabed.

**Squid**
A type of ten-armed mollusc related to the octopus. A squid seizes prey with its arms. To swim, water is forced out of the body through a narrow tube. This causes the squid to shoot quickly backwards.

**Tubeworm**
A type of aquatic worm that lives in a tube it builds from mud or other material.

**Viper fish**
A deep-sea fish with huge fangs that look rather like the fangs of a viper.

# INDEX

References in bold type refer to illustrations.

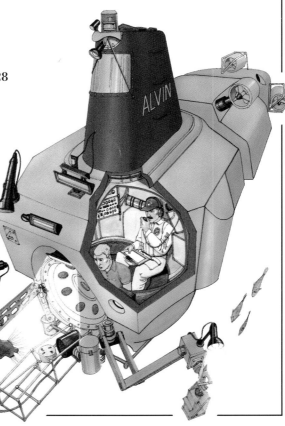